Alexey Bobrov

Easy Banjo Lessons

Express Course of Every Bluegrass Banjo Playing Technique + Online Video.
For Right-handed and Left-handed Players

The banjo photo on the cover — © Nmorozova / depositphotos
Picture design p. 1 — © Daniel Oravec / depositphotos

For any questions, comments or suggestions, email us at:
avgustaudartseva@gmail.com

CONTENTS

Introduction

Often in teaching books, the terms "right hand" and "left hand" are used to refer to the player's hands. In this edition, we will use the terms "lead hand (picking hand)" and "fingerboard hand" to avoid confusion.

For some right-handed players it may be more helpful to watch the left-handed version of the video (left-handed folks may likewise find the right-handed version more helpful). This has been shown to work well in face-to-face lessons.

This book will help you learn the basic techniques of playing the bluegrass banjo, read and play tablature, and play accompaniment using letter symbols.

Alexey Bobrov

Before You Start Playing

As you begin learning the banjo, you'll achieve the best results in as short of a time as possible if you use your lead hand for holding the pick. In this book, we'll cover all the specifics of playing for both right-handed and left-handed players.

First, put the thumb pick and the fingerpicks on the thumb and fingers of the lead hand. Then you pick up the banjo that's right for you.

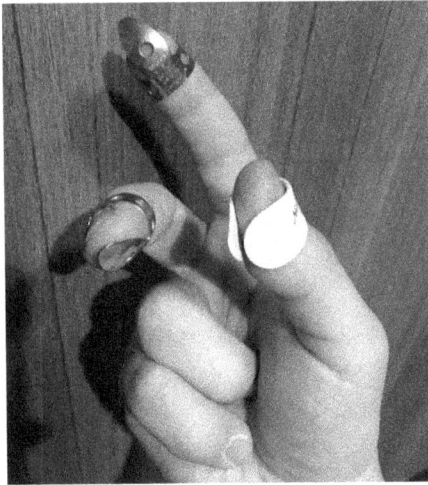

For right-handed players   For left-handed players

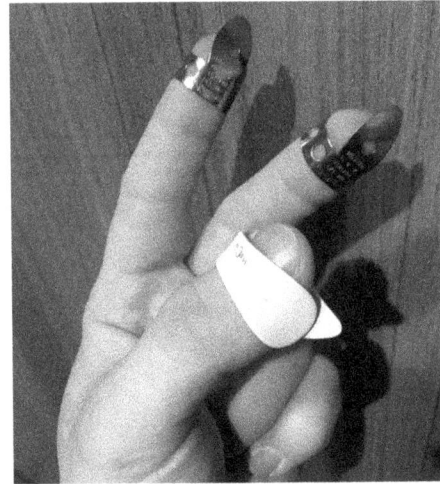

Metal fingerpicks are usually worn on the index and middle fingers while the thumb pick (commonly plastic) is placed on your thumb.

In addition to notes, tablature (tabs) is often used to play the banjo. In this tablature, the fingerings are represented by the following letters:

T — Thumb;
I — Index finger;
M — Middle finger.

To avoid confusion, remember that the shortest string on any banjo is the fifth string.

Before tuning a new banjo for the first time, especially if it has been shipped to you, you should check the position of the bridge. Measure the distance from the top nut to the end of the 12th fret (that's the metal strip after the two dots on the fingerboard). It should measure a little over 13 inches. The same distance should be measured from this metal strip to the bridge. All these measurements should be taken using the first string.

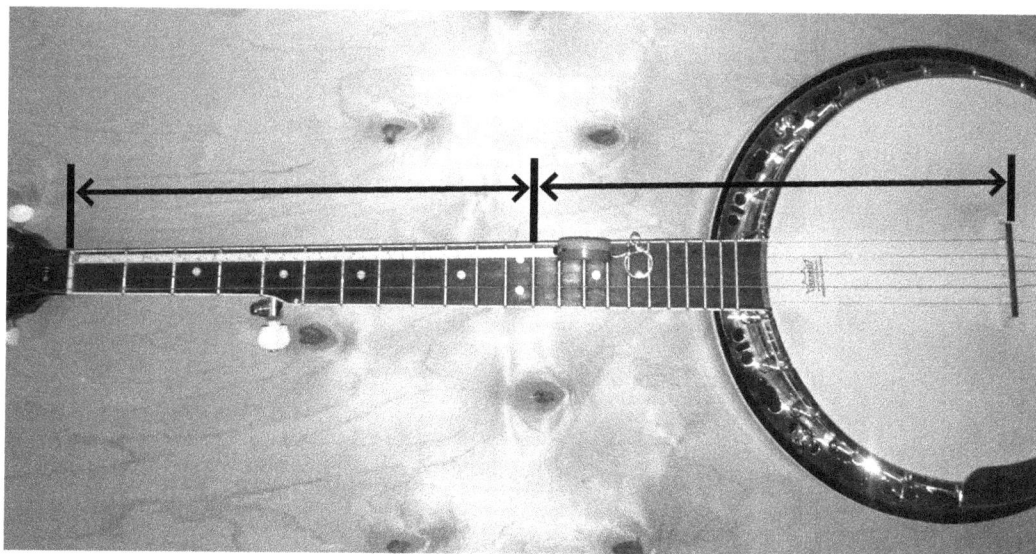

Tuning a Banjo

Now let's move on to tuning the instrument. To avoid confusing the string numbers, remember that the fifth string is the shortest string of all.

the 1st string — D;
the 2nd string — B;
the 3rd string — G;
the 4th string — D;
the 5th string — G.

On the piano, these sounds can be found on the following keys:

Piano Sheet Music Notation and Banjo Sheet Music Notation

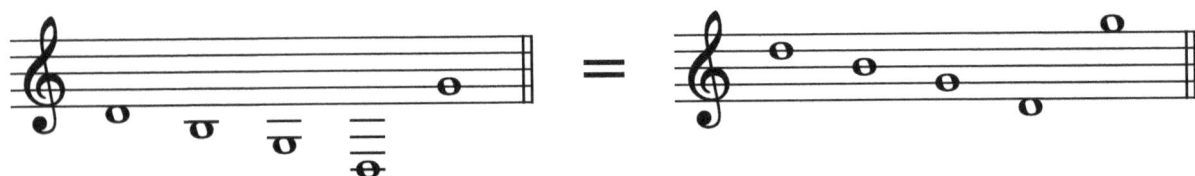

If you don't have a piano nearby, you can use a tuner, including a tuning app on your smartphone.

Start tuning from the first string. To avoid popping a string, do not twist the peg too fast, especially when you are coming close to the right pitch.

It is important to know that the banjo will hold its tuning better if the last move was toward tensioning the string rather than loosening it.

If the string doesn't hold its tension even for a second, tighten the screw on the tuning peg just a little. Don't tighten it too much though, otherwise the string might not hold the pitch at all!

If your banjo does not get in tune on the top frets even when the bridge has been adjusted, you may need to adjust the truss rod (if the distance between the strings and the fretboard is too great). This adjustment may require a visit to your local professional guitar shop.

Lead Hand Placement

Sit up straight and place the banjo between your legs. The neck of the banjo should not be in a horizontal position. Hold it at an angle of about 45 degrees.

Down at the bridge place your little finger straight up and place the weight of your hand on it. Your forearm will rest on the special plate. The picking hand has only two points of support — the forearm, which presses the banjo against your body, and the little finger, which stays in place.

There are two main approaches to lead hand placement. One is to rest only the little finger on the banjo head, and the other is to rest the little and ring finger on the head. We strongly recommend using only the little finger. This way the free ring finger will not constrain and slow down the movement of the middle finger, making it easier to achieve a fast tempo throughout the piece.

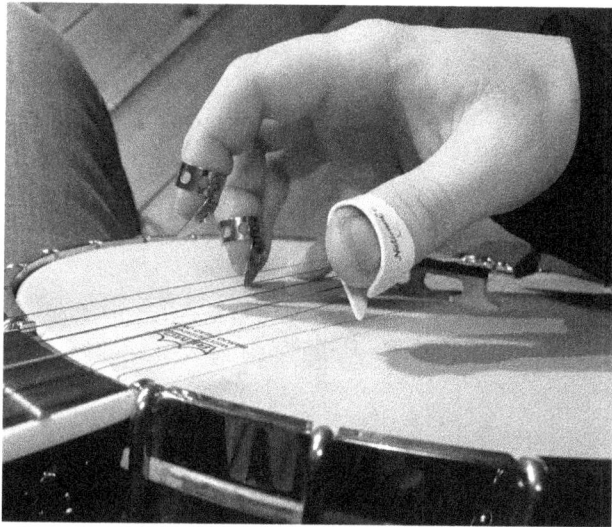

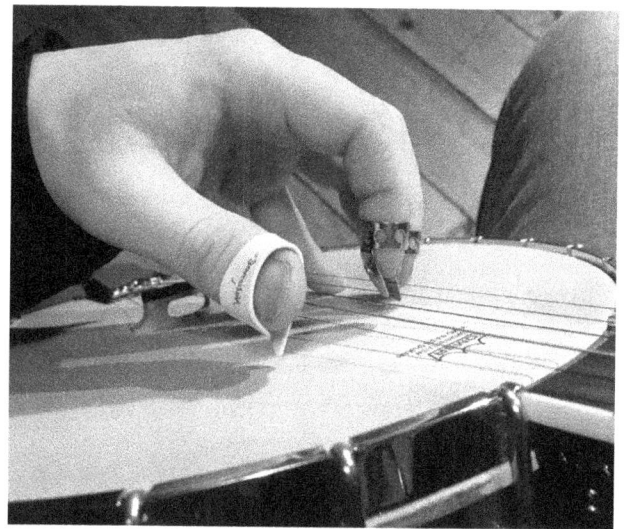

Be sure that your wrist should be bent toward the side of the banjo! Avoid a straight wrist (a flat hand position). See the wrong way to play (the wrist is straight) below:

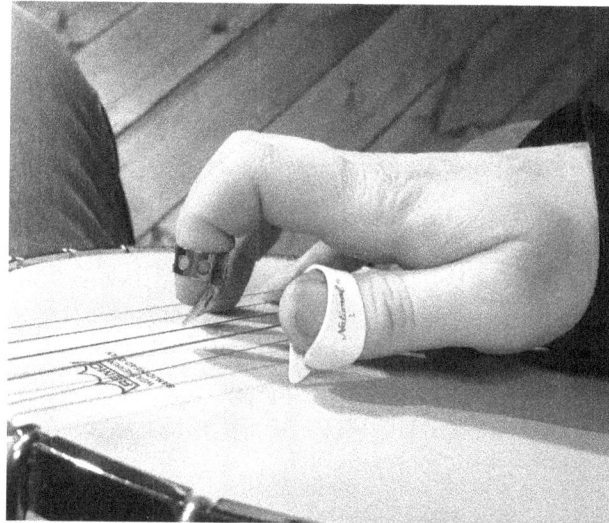

The middle finger will most often pluck the 1st string (pulling from bottom to top).

Index finger will pluck the 2nd and 3rd strings (pulling from bottom to top).

Thumb will pluck the 5th, 4th, 3rd, 2nd strings (pulling from top to bottom).

Tablature

Tabs (tablatures) are universal for both right and left-handed people. Let's look at an example of 4-note tabs and try to play them.

Here you see a diagram of 5 strings. The 5th string is the shortest. On the banjo it is located at the top, not at the bottom of the instrument, as it could appear from the diagram. In fact, it will be convenient for you if you arrange the tabs according to the setup of the strings — see the video for an example.

The zero stands for an open string (when you don't press any strings on the fingerboard).

The tabs are read from left to right. The first digit is on the 3rd string, so you should start by pulling it with the thumb, as indicated by the letter T above the digit. Next, play the open 2nd string with the index finger, followed by the 5th string with the thumb again. The last note is the open 1st string, played with the middle finger.

In the video, observe the firm position of the little finger, and focus on playing this exercise smoothly without any breaks. Ensure that all the notes are of equal length.

For right-handed players

For left-handed players

Important: When you pull the string with your index finger, make sure it doesn't hit your thumb afterwards. If this happens, try to keep the thumb away from the index finger.

Also, do not let the fingerpick brush against the banjo head. If this happens, insert the picks deeper onto the fingers and set the little finger more straight up (increase the distance to the head).

Hand Placement on the Fingerboard

To indicate the placement of the fingers on the fingerboard, lowercase letters are used. You are already familiar with "t", "i", "m", as well as "r", which stands for the ring finger, and "l" for the little finger.

There are 4 important rules to follow when placing your hand on the fingerboard:

1. There should always be a gap between your thumb and index finger (highlighted in the photo). Thanks to this rule, you will be able to play in a fast tempo without difficulty.

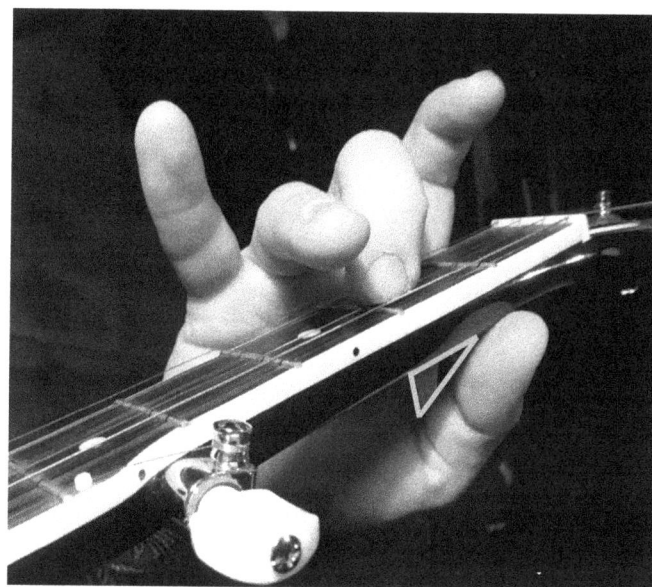

2. Your elbow should be under the fingerboard. This will help you reach the 4th string with your little finger and overall help you press the strings more easily.

3. When pressing a string, your finger should not touch the neighboring strings. Very often, when you press the 3rd string with your finger, the 2nd string is also touched. To avoid this, move your elbow more under the fingerboard.

4. When pressing the fret, place your finger closer to the top nut (the one that is closer to the picking hand, you can observe this in the video on page 15).

Using the following exercise, you will be able to check if your hand placement is correct (neighboring strings should sound good).

Place your middle finger on the second fret of the third string. Then, using your right hand, play what you played last time. This is what it looks like on the tabs:

```
     T  I  T  M
-1-----------0------
-2------0-----------
-3---2-------------
-4-----------------
-5------0----------
```

The Slide

Now let's get familiar with the "Slide" technique. This is when you pluck the string once and then slide the finger up or down the fingerboard to the other fret. Most often the slide is played upwards, such as sliding from the 2nd to the 3rd fret. Try playing the slide using a familiar fretting pattern:

Try playing all three examples exactly as you see in the video.
At the end, add the open 4th string and then simultaneously the 1st and 5th strings. This is what it looks like on the tabs:

The notes that are joined at the bottom last about half a second and are called eighth notes (given that a whole note lasts about 4 seconds). Those notes that are written separately last about 1 second (they are called quarter notes).

You may notice that when you slide, each of the two notes will sound shorter than the others (1/4 second for each) — these notes are called sixteenth notes. A large number of sixteenth notes is joined together with two horizontal lines at the bottom.

Look at the hand on the fingerboard from different angles and listen to the tempos of eighth, sixteenth, and quarter notes.

For right-handed players   *For left-handed players*

Try applying the slide to a very popular roll (the hand on the fingerboard uses only the middle finger):

1

2

The Hammer-on

The next fretting technique in terms of difficulty is called the hammer-on. When using this technique, you must play two notes while plucking the string once. It is usually played with an increase in pitch, as you were already doing when playing the slide.

First, play the open strings and get the correct rhythm. The first four notes are called eighths (1/8). The following notes that sound twice as long — quarters (1/4).

Using the lead hand, keep the same rhythm, but now, when you get to the first pluck of the string, add a middle finger strike on the second fret:

The first two notes now sound shorter. They are called sixteenths (1/16).

The middle finger strike on the fingerboard should come down with some force.

Keep in mind that you will lose some of the intensity of the sound when your finger strikes the string, so try to pluck the string louder. Do not extend the hammer-on effect too much and play almost immediately after plucking the string.

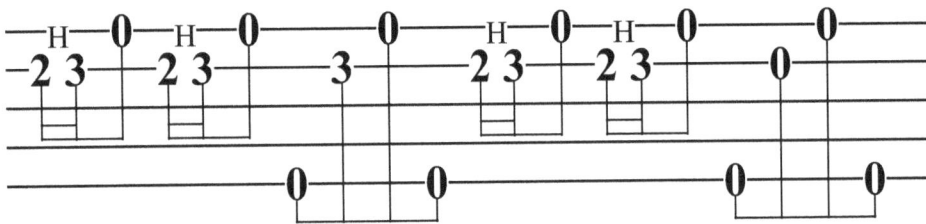

For right-handed players   *For left-handed players*

You have looked at an example of hammer-on using an open string.

Now try performing this technique on a closed string. This time, instead of the middle finger, you will be using the ring finger.

Note that the 1st and 3rd string plucks are played with different fingers (this is for convenience when playing fast).

For right-handed players   *For left-handed players*

18

The Pull-off

When performing the pull-off technique, you pull the string once, then, using your other hand, take one finger off the string so that there are two sounds.

There are a few tricks that will make your pull-off sound good:
1. Pull the string harder than usual so that the second note of the pull-off can be heard.
2. Release your finger almost immediately after pulling the string.
3. Bend the string a little so that the pull-off sounds brighter.

In tabs, pull-off is designated by the letter P.
Which way should you bend the string? This depends on the particular point at which the pull-off occurs. Let's consider two possibilities, since you will have to use two types of bends when playing. In both cases, the bend will be minimal, with almost no change in tone.

In the first case, you put both fingers on the 3rd string (middle and ring finger), so as not to drown out the 2nd string. Then you make a small bend towards the 4th string with the ring finger (you can use two fingers at the initial stages):

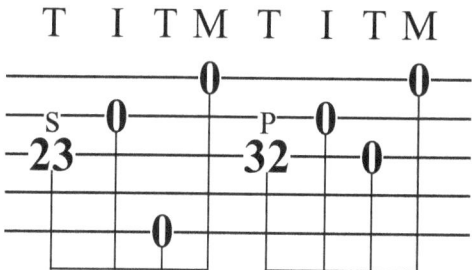

For right-handed players   *For left-handed players*

In the second case, you perform the pull-off on the open 3rd string and then make a bend towards the 2nd string. You should use your middle finger to play the pull-off instead of the ring finger:

For right-handed players   *For left-handed players*

Next, we will discuss the classic bend technique. It is always performed with the string shifted toward the higher numbered side, as in the first case. The second case of the bend is only performed when a pull-off is executed on an open string. The slight tension on the string during the pull-off cannot be called a true bend.

Up the Neck

To add variety to the sound of the banjo when playing at the top of the fingerboard, the picking hand is often moved away from the bridge closer to the center of the string. This changes the tone (or color) of the sound.

Play the progression in the usual way and then move the hand and play it again.

For right-handed players   *For left-handed players*

Bend

The classic bend is often performed higher up the neck. You will always move the string upward, toward the short 5th string.

Place your hand on the fingerboard (index and ring fingers). Perform the bend using the ring finger: the sound will have to blend in with the sound of the note that you have pressed with the index finger.

A rest (before the 16th fret) will be used in this example — it lasts a quarter note.

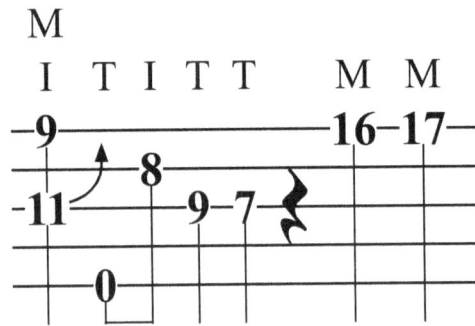

For right-handed players *For left-handed players*

Note that a barely noticeable bend is used on the 16th and 17th frets to make the notes sound clean (this is not usually specified in tabs). In the video, the bend is only done on the 16th fret and remains tense when you press the 17th fret, which you don't have to bend anymore. Fretted instruments do not always sound clean on the upper fret, even with a properly placed bridge.

Now look at another classic bend, but with a slide in front of it:

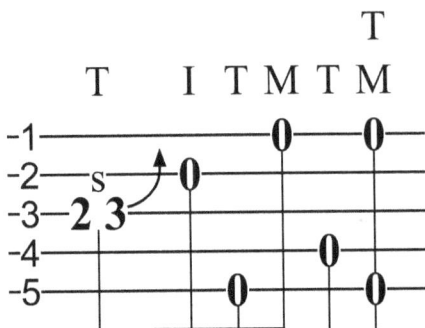

22

For right-handed players

For left-handed players

A Note on Tabs

Tabs can often vary in their notation. As an example, a slide or a hammer-on will be labeled with a slur or a slanted line.

Very often, the note that is played immediately after the slide/hammer-on is written at the same time as the second digit of the slide/hammer-on.

To avoid confusion, keep in mind this example, where two licks are very similar but different in spelling and sound.

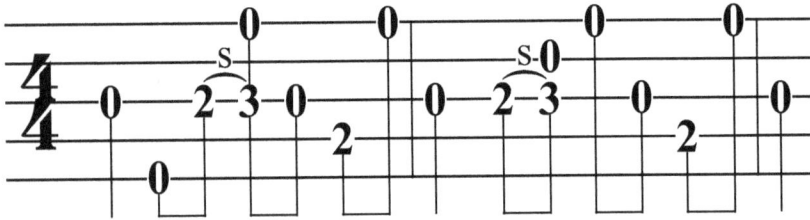

The four-four time signature at the beginning of the piece indicates that in each measure (or bar), there will be four quarter notes or eight eighths. In the example above, there are two full bars, and the last one is cut off after the first quarter. In the video example, each quarter is tapped with the foot, resulting in 4 beats per bar.

For right-handed players   *For left-handed players*

Also, the pull-off is sometimes indicated by a separate crossed-out note — always focus on the letter P, which denotes the pull-off technique.

Eliminating Rattling

When you play the banjo, you may hear foreign sounds such as rattling or buzzing. Often these can be eliminated on your own without needing to visit a guitar shop. Check all the troubleshooting points that go from simple to more complex:

1) Sometimes the buttons on the sleeve or hem of a shirt may be touching the instrument and rattle. So can belt buckles, bolo ties, chains, brooches, and metal badges.

2) If you play sitting down without a strap (usually it is used when playing standing up), the empty lug where the strap would be attached may be rattling. If this is the case, place a piece of duct tape over it.

3) The screws from the tuning pegs may have come loose a bit. This often happens with the 5th string peg. In this case, you don't even have to reach for a screwdriver — simply use your metal fingerpick. If you end up using a screwdriver, don't tighten too much, as it may block the mechanism and prevent the string from tightening.

4) Check the screws on the tailpiece and resonator. Make sure that the bridge is installed without tilting and that its feet are fully resting on the drum surface.

5) If the string rattles against the fret when playing open strings, then cut a piece of paper and place it under one, two or three legs of the bridge depending on the string. If the first string is rattling, then place a piece of paper under the foot that's located under that string. Look at the photo:

You can't usually see the paper, so feel free to add 2 pieces if one wasn't enough.

6) If rattling happens when a fret is pressed, place a piece of tin foil under the string on the nut. The photo shows how you can fix the 1st string rattling when the fret is clamped.

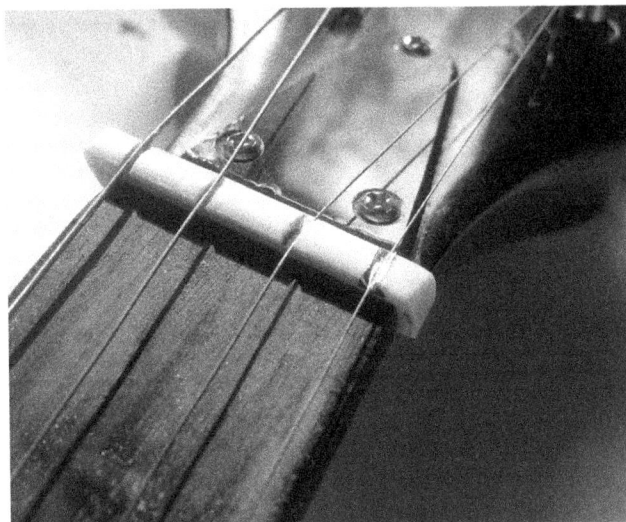

7) If, after completing all of these steps, you still hear a rattling sound, you may need to replace the string(s). If that doesn't resolve the issue, you might need to adjust the truss rod. Please note that truss rod adjustments can be tricky, so it's often best to visit your local professional guitar shop for assistance.

Accompaniment

An accompaniment is usually indicated by letters and numbers above the staff, tabs, or song lyrics.

Major chords are indicated by capital letters: A, B, C, D, E, F, G. Minor chords are labeled with an added lowercase letter m, for example: Am, Bm, Cm and so on.

If any sound is added to a chord, it is denoted by a number, which indicates the distance of that note from the main note (or the root) of the chord, e.g. Am4, B7...

In bluegrass music, the time signatures are often in 2/4 and 4/4, commonly known as two-four and four-four time. The following two examples of the G chord show fingerstyle playing in a typical bluegrass rhythm. These examples will sound the same whether you play them slowly in 2/4 time or quickly in 4/4 time.

G

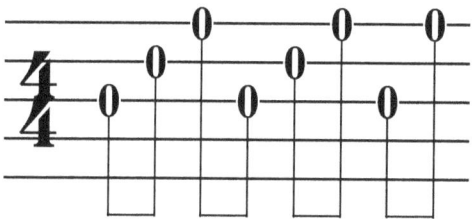

G

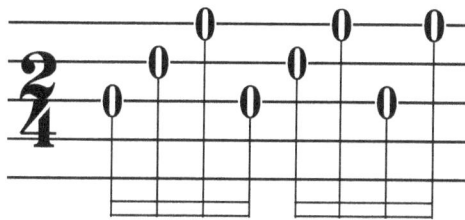

This is why the following examples will be given without rhythmic pattern so as not to visually complicate the notation.

Chord progression using the D, A7, G, and A chords:

D
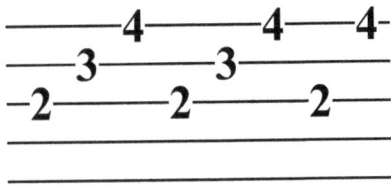

D
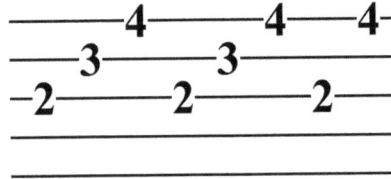

D
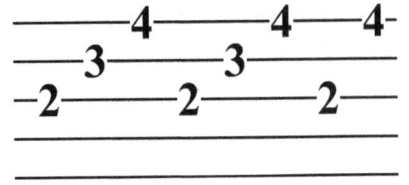

A7
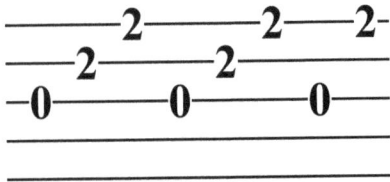

D
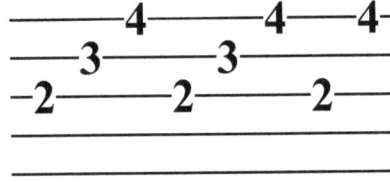

G
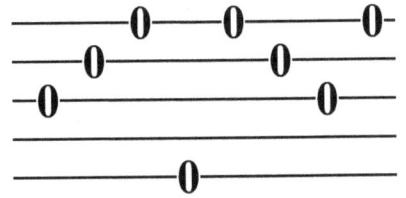

D   **A**   **D**
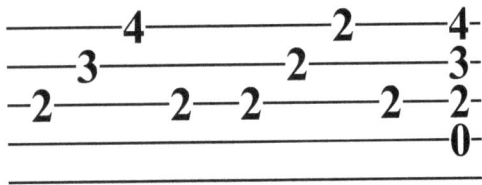

For right-handed players

For left-handed players

Next chord progression is C, E, Em, F, A7, Dm, G, Gm, A♯ / B♭:

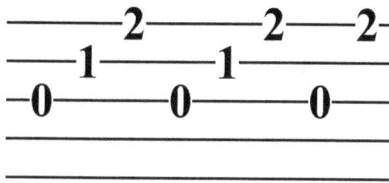

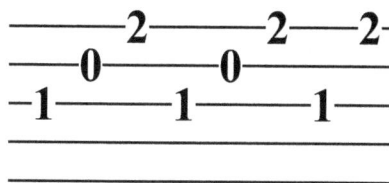

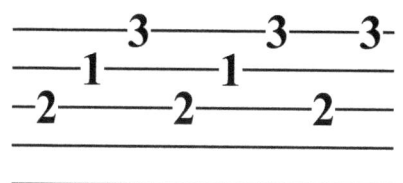

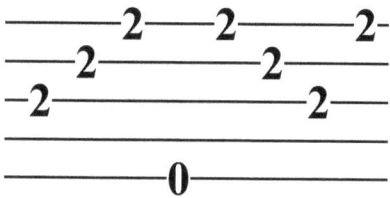

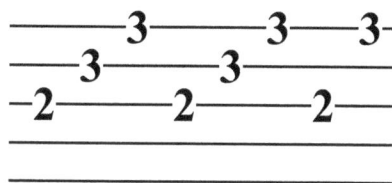

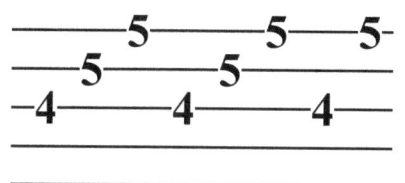

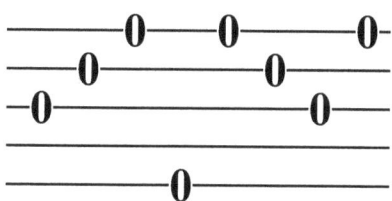

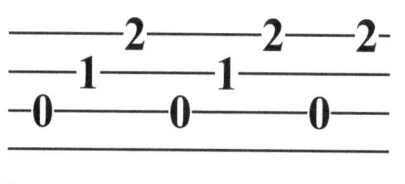

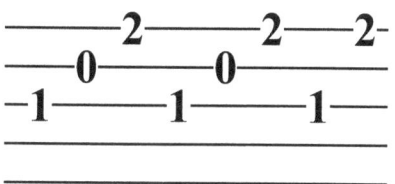

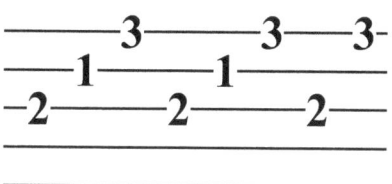

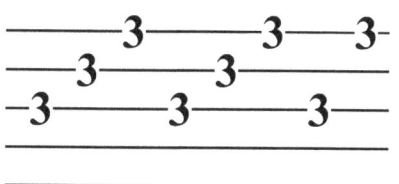

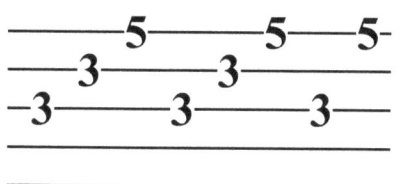

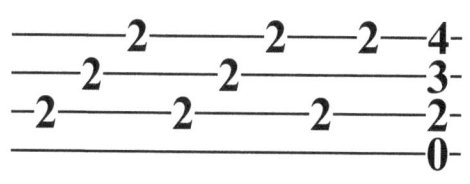

For right-handed players   *For left-handed players*

Try playing this chord progression — C, Am4 and G:

C

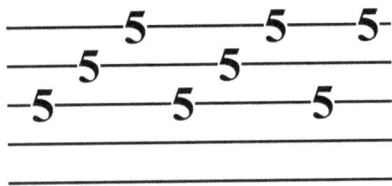

C

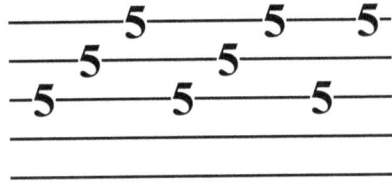

Am4

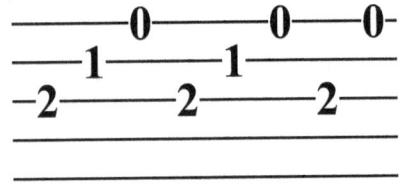

G

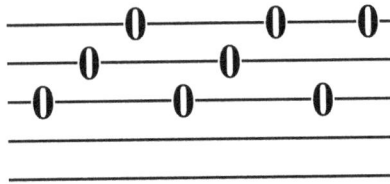

Now play the same progression, but with a few minor changes:

C

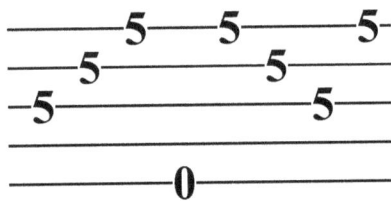

C

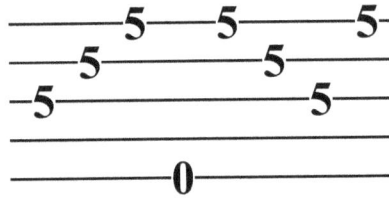

Am4

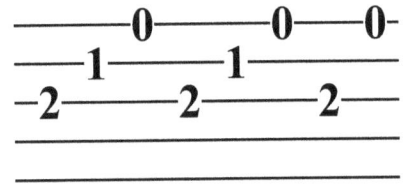

G

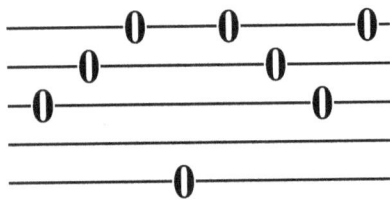

Now let's add some new chords:

C2

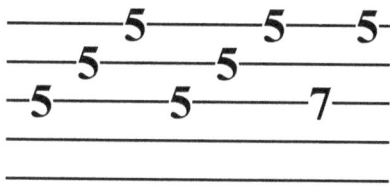

C2

Am7 add4 / Am7 (4)

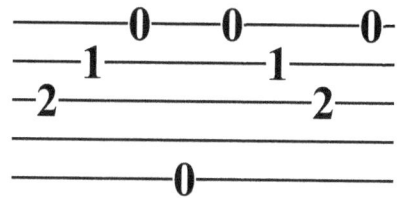

G7

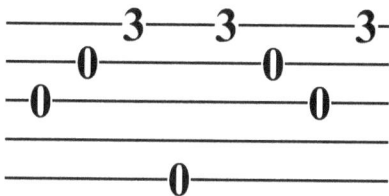

In the video, it sounds like this:

C   C   Am4   G
C   C   Am4   G
C2   C2   Am7 add4   G7   C2

For right-handed players   *For left-handed players*

Playing these chord sequences will teach you how to change chords. This will help you make your own chord variations and chord order. For fast chord progressions, begin finger placement by starting on the thickest string, moving from the 4th to the 1st string.

In the following example, consider a chord progression where some chords are held for a shorter duration.

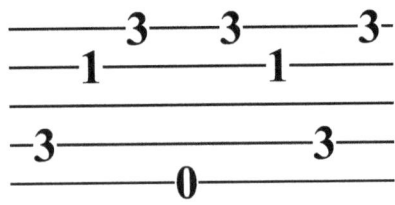

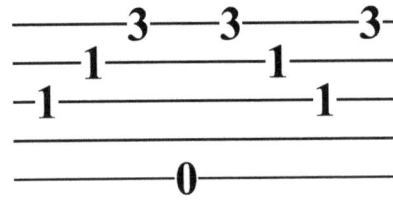

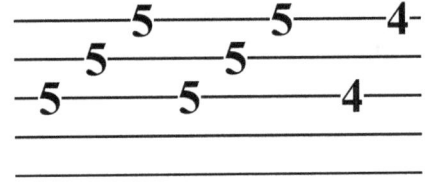

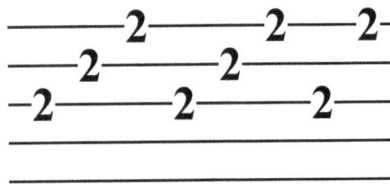

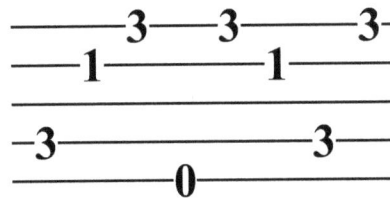

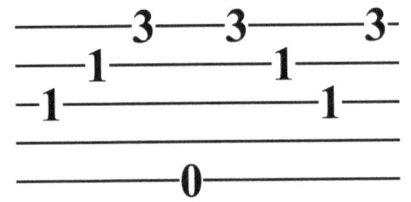

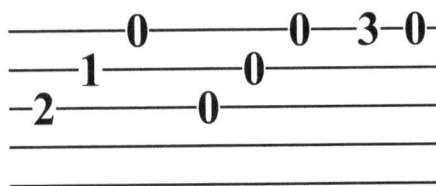

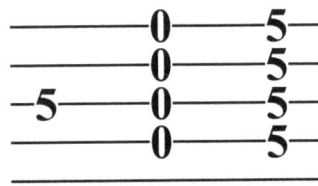

For right-handed players   *For left-handed players*

Look at the following example. Note the different variations of the Em chord. However, it is best to play them using the same fingers on the fingerboard. Start by placing your hand on the fingerboard as shown in the second Em variation.

F7
```
———3—3———3-
—1————1——
-3————————3—
————0——————
```

B
```
————4———4—4-
—4————4——
-4————4———4—
———————————
```

Em
```
————2—2———2-
—0————0——
———————————
-0——0———0—
```

Em
```
————2—2———2-
—0————0——
-2—————————
———————0———0—
```

Am
```
————2———2—2-
—1——1————
-2————2———2—
———————————
```

Am4
```
———0———0—0-
—1——1————
-2————2———2—
———————————
```

Bm
```
————4———4—4-
—3————3——
-4————4———4—
———————————
```

Em
```
————2—2———2-
—0————0——
———————————
—0———0———0—
```

Am
```
————2———2—2-
—1——1————
-2————2———2—
———————————
```

Am4
```
———0———0—0-
—1——1————
-2————2———2—
———————————
```

Bm
```
————4———4—4-
—3————3——
-4————4———4—
———————————
```

E
```
————2———2—2-
—0————0——
-1————1———1—
———————————
```

Am
```
————2———2—2-
—1——1————
-2————2———2—
———————————
```

Am4
```
———0———0—0-
—1——1————
-2————2———2—
———————————
```

G
```
———0—0———0-
—0————0——
-0————————0—
————0———————
```

In the video example, the third line of chords is played twice. Note that on the last line, another open (third) string is played after the G chord.

For right-handed players

For left-handed players

All Videos (Playlist)

All videos are included in the same playlist on YouTube *(online):*

or you may use the following link:

cutt.ly/3ejNbeX8

For any questions, comments or suggestions, email us at:
avgustaudartseva@gmail.com

Conclusion

You have learned the basic chords that are most often found in accompaniment.

Once you know these chords, you can use them in many different ways, such as in a different tuning, where you can simply change the chord names.

Use a capo for banjo or ukulele and remember to tune the short string to match the sound of the 3rd string.

Below is a table that shows how chords will be named with different capo positions. For chords that have accidentals (sharp or flat), there are two possible chord names.

					Chord on open strings			
Without a capo	C	D	E	F	G	A	B	A♯ / B♭
Capo on the 1st fret	C♯ / D♭	D♯ / E♭	F	F♯ / G♭	G♯ / A♭	A♯ / B♭	C	B
Capo on the 2nd fret	D	E	F♯ / G♭	G	A	B	C♯ / D♭	C
Capo on the 3rd fret	D♯ / E♭	F	G	G♯ / A♭	A♯ / B♭	C	D	C♯ / D♭

Try playing the same familiar sequence in classical G tuning without a capo, and then play it tuned in A♯ / B♭ with a capo on the 3rd fret.

If you tune the banjo to the key of G, you will have the following chords: C, E, F, A7, Dm, Em, F, G, C.

Then, set the capo on the 3rd fret. You also need to tune the 5th string according to the sound of the 3rd string. Now, the third fret becomes a zero, and you can press the same chords again. However, they will now sound different and be called differently:

If tuned in A♯, the chords will be D♯, G, G♯, C7, Fm, Gm, G♯, A♯, D♯.

If tuned in B♭, the chords will be E♭, G, A♭, C7, Fm, Gm, A♭, B♭, E♭.

Remember, there is no difference between the sound of A♯ and B♭, so use one of the variants, or two letters at once through a slash: A♯ / B♭.

Taking long breaks between banjo lessons is not recommended. Practice at least once a week so that you don't forget what you've learned.

We wish you much success!

COMPLETE PIANO for Beginners

AVGUSTA UDARTSEVA

Theory and Practice
65 Songs + Video

Learning to play your favorite songs on the piano is easy!

Today, the piano is probably the most popular musical instrument in the world. Playing this instrument will give you an unforgettable experience.

The book contains musical theory, practical exercises, and 65 popular songs for adults.

ISBN: 979-8361128570

ASIN: B0BKYHL7PC

United States   United Kingdom   Canada

EASY RECORDER LESSONS for Kids

VIDEO AND AUDIO

60 Songs

First Book Step by Step

- Learning step by step: starting with more simple tunes, then gradually moving to more complex songs.
- Includes music theory, instrument history, practice, recommendations and many entertaining songs.
- Learn the position of the body and hands, how to breathe properly and play easily.
- Letters above each note and simple explanations.
- Convenient large US Letter print size.
- Video accompaniment to all lessons by direct link inside the book.
- 2-in-1 Book: Recorder lessons and video + 60 Songs.

And it's great for adults!

ISBN: 979-8386419004

ASIN: B0BXMX7ZVN

United States   United Kingdom   Canada

www.ingramcontent.com/pod-product-compliance
Lightning Source LLC
Chambersburg PA
CBHW081640040426

42449CB00014B/3390